BRUCE JENNER

DECATHLON WINNER

Nathan Aaseng

 Lerner Publications Company ■ Minneapolis

21680

To my wife, an excellent live-in editor

LIBRARY OF CONGRESS CATALOGING IN PUBLICATION DATA

Aaseng, Nathan
Bruce Jenner.

(The Achievers)
Includes index.
SUMMARY: A biography of the young American whose
four years of intense training enabled him to win the decathlon
at the 1976 Olympics.

1. Jenner, Bruce, 1949-   —Juvenile literature. 2. Track and
field athletes—United States—Biography—Juvenile literature.
3. Decathlon—Juvenile literature. 4. Olympic Games, Montréal,
Québec, 1976—Juvenile literature. [1. Jenner, Bruce, 1949-
2. Track and field athletes. 3. Decathlon] I. Title. II. Series.

GV697.J38A65 1979   796.4'2'0924 [B] [92]   79-4497
ISBN 0-8225-0477-4

Manufactured in the United States of America.

International Standard Book Number: 0-8225-0477-4
Library of Congress Catalog Card Number: 79-4497

3   4   5   6   7   8   9   10   90   89   88   87   86   85   84   83   82   81

Athletes from many nations carry their countries' flags into the Olympic stadium in Munich.

1

Bruce Jenner felt proud as he warmed up in the red, white, and blue uniform of the United States track team. This was the Olympics!

Thousands of years ago, the strongest and fastest men from various Greek tribes and cities met in the first Olympics. They had stopped their wars long enough to race and wrestle and to throw the discus. The modern Olympics still hold these ancient events, as well as many newer ones. Every four years, the world's best amateur athletes — both men and women — gather to show their skills in the Olympics. This year Bruce was one of them.

What a thrill it was for Bruce to take part in the Olympics! But it was also terrifying. As Bruce lined up for the first race of the decathlon, he saw great athletes on both sides of him. They were so good at the decathlon, they could make even a good athlete look silly. And the crowds were so huge! Millions more were watching the Olympics on television. It was enough to scare the bravest of athletes.

Bruce tried not to think of anything but doing his best. He ran the races as fast as he could, but there were people competing who ran faster. He jumped and threw as far as he could, but he saw others throwing and jumping much farther. When the decathlon events were over, Bruce knew that he had done his best, but that there were others who had done even better.

Now that the Olympics were over for Bruce, he could sit in the stands and watch others prove their skills. Soon the scoreboard would show the results of the decathlon. Bruce knew that he had not come close to winning a medal. A tall, tanned Russian named Nikolai Avilov had surprised many experts by winning the decathlon. Earlier, one of the largest sports magazines in the United States had printed the names of the athletes who they thought would win the top three places in the decathlon. They had not

Russian decathlon winner Nikolai Avilov pole vaulting in the
1972 Olympics

picked Avilov to win any of the three.

But Avilov had waited until the most important time of all—the Olympics—to show what he could do. Bruce had seen the Russian's grace as he sailed over the high-jump bar and floated over the hurdles. Avilov could do everything, it seemed. He was an ideal athlete for the decathlon: a one-man track team.

The decathlon actually is ten events rolled into one. In fact, the name *decathlon* comes from two Greek words meaning "ten" and "sports contest." The decathlon tests the three things that make up all the events in track: running, jumping, and throwing. Four of the events in the decathlon are running races. The 100-meter (110-yard) race is a *sprint*. A sprint is a race in which an athlete runs at top speed for a short distance. The 1,500-meter race is nearly a mile long. Those who run it must learn to pace themselves and keep running even when they get tired. The 400-meter (440-yard) race falls somewhere between sprinting and long-distance running. Some athletes think of the 400 meter as a very long sprint. The fourth race is the hurdles, in which runners speed over 10 evenly spaced hurdles. (Hurdles are like fences 3½ feet, or about 1 meter, high.)

There are three jumping events: the long jump, the high jump, and the pole vault. Long jumpers run down a hard path and jump from a board as far as they can into a sand pit. High jumpers must jump over a bar without knocking it down. The pole vault is like the high jump, except that athletes use a pole to carry them over the bar.

The shot put, the discus, and the javelin make up the three throwing events. In the shot put, the athlete throws a heavy iron ball. This event calls for a great deal of strength. The discus and javelin (spear) are not so heavy. They call for as much skill as muscle. One must do well in all 10 events to win the gold medal, awarded for first place in the Olympic decathlon.

Decathlon scoring is not simple. Points are awarded depending on how well an athlete does in each of the 10 events. Scoring is based on how close an athlete comes to the existing world record. It is always possible for an athlete to top the world record, so there is really no limit to the number of points an athlete can score in any given event.

Bruce looked up as the colorful lights on the scoreboard flashed the results. First place: Avilov of Russia with 8,454 points (a new world record). Second: Litvinenko of Russia. Third: Katus of Poland. Bruce had to wait a while to see his name. There it was. Tenth place: Jenner of the United States.

Well, Bruce sighed, he was lucky just to be there. He had shocked even himself by winning the last spot on the United States' decathlon team. Bruce was young. He knew his body would be in its best shape four years from then. That's when the next Olympics would be. "I know I can do better," he thought. Then he made a decision. He would spend the next four years doing just one thing: becoming the world's greatest decathlon performer.

Many people who watched Jenner perform in those Olympics in Munich in 1972 did not think that he had much of a chance. Tenth place in the Olympics was a very good finish. But it was a long way behind the man wearing the gold medal — Nikolai Avilov.

2

It came as no surprise to the people of Tarryton, New Jersey, that young Bruce Jenner was good at sports. It ran in the family. His father and grandfather both had been good athletes. Besides that, young Bruce seemed strong almost from the day he was born. Throughout high school, he had taken part in all kinds of sports: wrestling, football, basketball, and track. Most of all, he loved waterskiing.

When the Jenners moved to Connecticut, a track coach there noticed how good Bruce was at every sport he tried. The way Bruce could run, jump, and pole vault showed that he would be perfect for another kind of sport: the decathlon. Bruce was just the person L. D. Weldon was looking for, thought the coach.

Mr. Weldon worked for Graceland College, which was in a small town in Iowa. He loved the decathlon, and he was always looking for promising young athletes whom he could turn into decathlon champions. Mr. Weldon talked to Bruce over the phone, and, before Bruce knew it, he had signed up to go to the tiny college a thousand miles from home.

Even though Graceland wanted him for the decathlon, Bruce tried other sports. Poor Mr. Weldon could hardly bear to watch as Bruce went through his crunching football drills that fall. What if Bruce hurt himself playing football and would never be able to run the decathlon? Bruce won a spot on the football team playing defense, and, sure enough, he hurt his knee. He hurt it so badly that he thought he might have to quit sports forever. Luckily, the knee healed, but it kept him out of action for several months.

Because of his knee, Bruce still had not run a decathlon by the time school ended that year. He did not know if he ever would. A job waiting for Bruce in Florida sounded better to him than college. He would be teaching waterskiing and performing for tourists there.

That May, while driving from a friend's house in Virginia, Bruce tried to decide what he should do. He could go home for the summer and return to college in the fall. Or he could take the road to Florida. He was still deciding, when a car moved up and blocked the turning lane to the highway that would take him to Florida. Bruce could have slowed down behind the car and taken the turn. But somehow he didn't feel like bothering, so he went home. At the summer's end, Bruce wound up going back to school — all because he had been too lazy to get into the turning lane for Florida!

The next spring, Bruce finally started work on the decathlon. After just one month of practice, his coach entered him in the Drake Relays. "What a way to start!" Bruce must have thought. The famous Drake Relays is a huge track meet held in Des Moines, Iowa. College runners and older expert track people from all over the country gather at the Relays to see how well they can do. Thousands of athletes attend, some of them world record holders.

Entering the Drake Relays was a rough way to start. But because Bruce had always thrown and jumped well, even without much practice, he scored almost 7,000 points in his very first try at the Drake Relays — more than anyone from Graceland had ever scored.

What was more, Bruce liked the decathlon. It's always fun to be good at something, and in the decathlon, Bruce was good at nearly everything. He also liked being able to do everything himself. The decathlon was not like football, in which you could do a good job and still lose because others had not done their jobs well. Bruce always tried to do a good job and had only himself to blame when things went poorly in the decathlon.

Bruce's athletic life was getting better, and so was his personal one. At Graceland, he met Chrystie Crownover, an attractive blonde student. Before long, they were married.

With practice, Bruce improved in the decathlon and won a few large meets. In one of his last college track meets, Bruce scored enough points to try out for the U.S. Olympic team. He was thrilled at the chance to go to the Olympic try-outs, which would be held in Eugene, Oregon. The top three athletes in every event at the trials would wear the U.S. colors at the Olympics!

Bruce knew that he was still learning, and he did not expect to win a place on the team. His parents did not even think it worth the trouble to go to Oregon to watch. Still, Bruce gave it all he had. With one event to go (the 1500-meter race), he found himself in fifth place. Not bad. But wait! If he could beat the two men just ahead of him by 18 seconds,

Bruce Jenner in the 1,500-meter event of the decathlon during the 1972 Olympic trials

he would finish third and win a spot on the U.S. Olympic team headed for the 1972 games in Munich! He would have to run his best ever to do it.

Bruce looked over at his two opponents, who seemed tired. "I can do it!" he thought. He was so excited before the race that he was jumping up and down while the others were gulping air. He could hardly wait for the race to start!

When the starting gun went off, Bruce bounded past the two men whom he had to beat. Halfway through the race, they still hung right behind him. But as Bruce ran faster and faster, the two dropped farther behind. Bruce chased his goal with the fierce, fiery need to win that had always amazed onlookers. He wanted a place on the U.S. Olympic team so badly that when he crossed the finish line, he had beaten his opponents by 21 seconds. He had done it! Bruce had also broken his own personal record by running 8 seconds faster than he had ever run before.

Bruce Jenner surprised everyone by winning the trip to the 1972 Olympics. And his 10th place finish at those games only made him hungrier than ever to become the best. It was the start of the long, hard drive that he hoped would win him the gold medal in 1976.

3

Now that he was out of college, Bruce found that it was harder than ever to train. He still could work out at Graceland and use the college's equipment. But he no longer had any scholarship, and he needed to make enough money to live. Nobody pays an athlete to practice the decathlon in the United States, so Bruce made money during the next four years by trimming tree branches and selling insurance. There would never have been enough to live on had it not been for his wife, Chrystie. She worked for an airline, supporting the two of them so that Bruce could spend most of his time training.

Winter was another problem. Bruce always wanted to be outdoors, working out. But it was no fun to practice running and jumping in the bitter cold, snow, and ice of an Iowa winter. The Jenners solved many problems by moving to California. In San Jose, their new hometown, the weather was nice enough for residents to be outside all year long.

Many other fine track people had moved to that town for the same reason. Bruce was able to watch them and to make many friends among them. When he saw how good some of them were, Bruce knew he had a long way to go before he could be satisfied with his performance. It wasn't long before the country's top jumpers and discus throwers were showing Bruce some of their secrets. These expert athletes were the best coaches he could have found.

Bruce worked hard. He even set up a hurdle in his living room! Every time Bruce went through the room, even if he was just going to turn on the television, he practiced going over the hurdle. Sometimes Chrystie would find him trying to run while he slept at night. He was dreaming about training. His mind and body did not even want to take time out for sleeping!

The decathlon became more and more important to Bruce. He no longer had time for trimming trees and waterskiing. He only had time for training. Because there are so many events in the decathlon, many different skills are required. For Bruce, there never seemed to be time enough to practice any of them really well. A few throws of the javelin would just start to feel good when it was time to quit that and pull on the running shoes.

The decathlon is a very strange sporting event, in that it is bad for an athlete to be too good at any one part of it. That sounds silly, but it's true. If Bruce had practiced running the long 1,500-meter race too much, his legs would not be used to the short, fast races. Or if he had lifted weights for hours to build huge muscles for the shot put, he would be too heavy to high jump. He might even break the pole if he tried to pole vault!

There was a Chinese athlete named C. K. Yang who found this out the hard way. In the 1952 Olympics, Yang was such a fantastic athlete that he beat everyone in 7 out of the 10 decathlon events. Rafer Johnson, an American, won only one event, the shot put. Yang was the easy winner, right? Wrong! For all his talent, Yang had trouble throwing. He finished far behind in the three throwing events. Johnson had "balance." This means that he was not super in many events, but that he was good in *all* of them. He stayed close to the top in the events that Yang won and destroyed him in the throwing events. As a result, Johnson walked away with the gold medal.

Bruce makes a good toss in the discus event of the decathlon at a 1975 meet with Russia and Poland.

Bruce gets a hug from Chrystie after winning the decathlon and setting a new world record in 1975.

After a while, Bruce's hard work in each of the decathlon events really began to pay off. He won most of the decathlons that he entered. Then he scored more than 8,000 points, something very few people have ever done. But that was nothing compared to what happened in 1975, when he ran against Avilov in a track meet in Oregon. Not only did Bruce beat the Russian, but he also broke his world record with a score of 8,524 points.

Ranked first in world decathlon competition, Bruce makes a good leap in the long jump at the 1976 U.S. Olympic trials.

When it came time for the trials for the 1976 Olympic team, it was a far different story from the 1972 trials. Now all the decathlon men were out to beat Bruce. And this time, all the fans were watching him from the start. What a treat he gave them! He broke the decathlon world record yet another time!

Bruce's dream of a gold medal was now more than a dream. After four hard years of work, he could challenge Avilov. Bruce would risk everything on that one decathlon in the 1976 Olympics. Win or lose, the Olympic games in Montreal, Canada, would be his *last* decathlon. There hc would find out if his and Chrystie's long years of effort had been worth it. This time, tenth place or third place or even second place out of all the decathlon men in the world would not be good enough. Bruce Jenner wanted the gold medal.

Time out for relaxation before the 1976 Olympic games

4

In the summer of 1976, Montreal meant just one thing to most of the world: the Olympics. For Bruce Jenner, Montreal meant the end of a way of life. Almost everything he had done during the previous four years had been done with Montreal in mind.

The days before he was to perform, Bruce tried to relax and get away from all the tension. He had Chrystie along for support, and they had even brought their yellow labrador, Bertha, with them. Bertha had always been able to help Bruce relax. But it was impossible for Chrystie and Bertha to keep Bruce's mind off the coming Olympics.

Avilov! Avilov! That name kept popping into Bruce's thoughts. One evening Chrystie and Bruce stood on a dock, looking over a peaceful Canadian lake. Chrystie hoped this peaceful setting would calm him. But while they were standing there, Bruce turned a half circle and flung out his arm. Even there, he was throwing a pretend discus!

Small worries suddenly seemed bigger. Bruce had stretched a muscle in his leg a few weeks earlier. It did not bother him now, but what if the pain returned? Worse yet, he had hurt his throwing hand — his left hand — while practicing the shot put at that year's Drake Relays. It hurt him so much that he could not throw hard. He was afraid that he would have to settle for a poor throw in the shot put. That would make the job of winning the decathlon even harder.

Then there was the waiting. The decathlon was not held until later in the Olympics, so Bruce could only watch the other athletes perform until his turn came. The pressure sometimes became unbearable. Bill Toomey had talked about this. Toomey was an American who had won the Olympic decathlon in 1968. "You can't believe how frightening it is until you have been there," he said. Toomey himself had hardly been able to stand the tension before he went out and won his gold medal in Mexico City in 1968. He had wanted to go home.

Bruce knew that Toomey's words were true. He was nearly bursting with tension and energy. It was all he could do to sit still. But he had to. He could not afford to waste his energy before he needed it.

What made the waiting worse was that Bruce's American teammates were not doing well that year in track. Many American stars were expected to win medals. Some of them were Bruce's good friends. He could hardly bear to sit by while his friends and teammates tried for their medals and failed. Bruce was anxious to make up for their losses.

Finally, the day came. The first group of runners was called in for the 100-meter (110-yard) dash. Athletes are always most nervous before the first event. But the 100-meter dash made them nervous for another reason. It is the shortest race in the decathlon, about as long as a football field from one goal line to the other. In the 100, time is very important; even tiny parts of a second can make a difference in the results of a race.

To find out how important time is to a runner in the 100-meter dash, try clapping your hands together twice, as fast as you can. Of two runners who start at the same time, the runner who finishes on the first clap gets about 50 points more than the runner who finishes on the second clap!

Because every moment is so important, all runners are very jumpy at the starting line. They lean forward and their muscles are so ready to run at the sound of the gun that sometimes they start too soon. When a runner starts too soon, it is called a *false start* and the race must be started again. Everyone is allowed one false start. More than one, and the runner is out of the race with no chance for a medal. Because there are usually many false starts, a runner never really knows which start will be the real race. He or she always has to be ready.

There were too many decathlon men at the Montreal Olympics to run all at once. So they were split into groups called *heats*. Avilov's heat would run first while Bruce finished his warm-up. Bruce figured that there were three men who might be able to beat him in the decathlon. Avilov, of course, was one. Bruce's American teammate, Fred Dixon, was another. The third was a new star from West Germany, Guido Kratschmer. Bruce would keep an eye on them.

Bruce saw Avilov start before the gun went off. One more false start, and Bruce's main rival would be out of the running before Bruce ever ran. Avilov had to be careful. More runners took false starts. When a true start finally came, Avilov was not quite as ready as he wanted to be. He started slowly and finished with a time of 11.23 seconds. Most of us would feel as speedy as roadrunners if we could run that fast. But for Avilov, it was a poor time.

Fred Dixon ran in the next heat. His time of 10.94 was slower than usual for him, too. Bruce's turn came next, and he settled his feet into the metal starting blocks. These blocks are pounded into the ground so that runners can push off from them at the start to keep their feet from slipping.

"Runners to your mark!" yelled the starter, holding a gun high. "Set!" BANG! The runners sprang forward and charged down the track. No false starts. Bruce lost ground to the man in the next lane, but he gained speed and crossed the finish line just behind him. Bruce's time of 10.94 tied Dixon's. He had not counted on being ahead of Avilov so soon. Maybe winning the gold medal would not be so hard.

No such luck. Guido Kratschmer raced in the last heat, and he was not just out for a Sunday stroll! His powerful legs rocketed him down the track in a time of 10.66. The decathlon was under way with Kratschmer well out in front.

"Jolting Jenner" competes in the shot-put event during Olympic decathlon competition in Montreal.

5

The next event was the long jump. One after the other, the decathlon athletes ran with long, high steps down the long-jump runway and jumped. After everyone had jumped once, Bruce found himself almost 19 inches (about 48 centimeters) behind both Avilov and Kratschmer. And those two had not even jumped well! Bruce did not have Kratschmer's speed to send him far into the pit. Nor could he hang in the air as long as Avilov.

On his second try, Avilov sailed far out into the sand pit, much farther than anyone had jumped yet. But a judge saw that Avilov's toe had crossed over the take-off line. That was a foul. Avilov's jump did not count. Kratschmer also fouled on his second leap.

Bruce did much better on his second try, but his jump did not count because a high wind at his back had helped him along.

When Bruce was called over for his third and final jump, he must have felt as if a heavy weight had fallen from his shoulders. Avilov and Kratschmer were already through jumping for the day. For some reason, neither had been able to top their first jumps. It was a good break for Bruce. He sprinted down the hard, narrow runway and leaped high, legs far forward. He stretched as far as he could and hit the sand with his heels more than 23½ feet (about 7 meters) away, his best jump ever! He still had not matched Avilov or Kratschmer, but that did not matter. Bruce had done what he wanted to by not falling far behind.

Fred Dixon, clearly off to a bad start, did not jump as far as he usually did. It was just another of the many unlucky things that would happen to him in this decathlon. Since Dixon was having problems, that left just Avilov and Kratschmer for Bruce to watch during the rest of the competition.

Bruce took off his sand-filled jumping shoes and pulled out his shot-putting shoes. On to the shot-put ring. He knew the order of events so well that he did not even have to think about it. He had done plenty of fretting about the shot put. How would his sore hand feel? He tucked the heavy steel ball against his chin — no muscles complained. As he crouched low in the shot-put ring, he knew that the hand had somehow healed.

The shot put calls for one second of pure power. Free from worry about his hand, Bruce let go with all his might. The last of Bruce's three throws fell to earth more than 50 feet (15 meters) away. That was more like it! It was his best toss ever! But when Avilov and Kratschmer walked away from the ring after throwing, they, too, were proud of themselves. Both of them had just finished their best shots ever, each more than 48 feet (14.4 meters)!

The high jump was the next decathlon event, and it was Avilov's favorite. It was not Bruce's. As in the long jump, Bruce could only hope to stay close in that event and to wait for his strong events, which were coming up the next day.

Kratschmer seemed too big and heavy to lift himself over the high jump crossbar. But the bearded German had practiced well. He hurled himself high and cleared a height of 6 feet 6 inches (almost 2 meters). Avilov and Jenner managed to do the same. The bar was raised two inches (about 5 centimeters) higher. Avilov knew he could easily clear that height, and he did not want to waste his strength on such "easy" jumps. So he put on his sweatsuit, sat down, and waited for the bar to be placed much higher. This must have made Kratschmer and Jenner feel unimportant. At 6 feet 8 inches (a little more than 2 meters), the bar was already higher than they had ever jumped before. And Avilov thought it was too easy! Both Bruce and Kratschmer missed their first two tries. Three misses in a row at any height and they would not be allowed to jump anymore.

On his last try, Kratschmer hit a perfect leap and made it over. The pressure was on Bruce. He ran toward the bar and jumped, twisting in the air. His head went over first, then his back. Last to come were his legs. It looked as if they would crash into the bar. But in the final instant, Bruce kicked just in time and his legs were over. Bruce hopped to his feet, raising his fist, a sign that he was pleased. On the day when it really counted, he was doing things that he had never done before.

Kratschmer and Bruce could go no higher. Avilov finally removed his sweatsuit and went to work. It was amazing how easily he sailed over the bar. Again and again the bar was inched higher, and Avilov always managed to soar over it. He was a fairly tall man, and the heights he was jumping were nearly a foot over his head! Would he ever miss? Finally he did, but his best jump of more than 7 feet (2.10 meters) put him ahead of Bruce.

The last event of the day was the 400-meter (440-yard) run. This race is a little longer than once around a football field. Avilov, Jenner, and Kratschmer were all scheduled for the same heat. Avilov had beaten Bruce in this event in 1972, but Bruce thought he could change that this time.

The first time you watch the 400-meter event, you may think that it looks as if someone is cheating. The runners in the outside lanes get to start way in front of the runners in the inside lanes (the lanes closest to the middle). The reason for this is that the outside lanes are longer, and no one is allowed to change lanes. So the runners on the outside start ahead so that they all run the same distance and finish in the same place.

Bruce started off inside of Avilov and Kratschmer. When the gun sounded, he could see them out in front of him. Avilov moved out quickly, but Bruce was ready for him. Before long, Bruce caught up to Avilov. The crowd saw how hard Bruce was running and cheered him on. Around the last turn, Bruce passed everyone. His muscles ached and his lungs fought for breath, but he refused to slow down. Bruce hit the finish line in first place! His time of 47.5 seconds

Crossing the finish line in the fourth heat of the 400-meter run

amazed track experts. Bruce had improved more than 100 points over his 1972 race!

When Bruce left the track, carrying his bag of shoes (a different pair for almost every event), much of his nervousness had left him. It did not bother him that at the end of the first day of the decathlon he was only in third place. Everyone knew how good Bruce Jenner was in the last four events. And his main worry was not Avilov or Kratschmer anymore. Even if they did their best, a good performance by Bruce would beat them. The only man who could defeat Bruce Jenner was Bruce Jenner! Bruce knew that he could defeat himself — by making just one mistake. One tiny mistake, and he would be in trouble again.

Unfortunately, the next day's events were the ones in which it was easy to take a wrong step. Bruce knew how easy it was to trip over a hurdle, or to miss in the pole vault, or to foul in the discus. Any one of these could cost him his gold medal. Little mistakes and bad luck had already ruined the hopes of many of his American teammates. Earl Bell and Dave Roberts had expected to win the top two places in the pole vault. All year long they had taken turns breaking the world pole-vault record as if there were nothing to it. But luck was not with them in the Olympics, and they had failed. So, too, would Dwight Stones, the world's best high jumper, and Frank Shorter, the world's top marathon runner. It did not matter how many thousands of hours they had practiced — something had still gone wrong.

If Bruce made the same kinds of mistakes, he would lose. If not, he was sure to win the gold medal.

Bruce clears the bar in the pole-vault event of decathlon competition.

6

The first challenge facing Bruce the next morning was the hurdles. It did not help matters when Fred Dixon, who was having a terrible decathlon, fell in the first heat. The fall cost Dixon hundreds of points in the hurdles. Besides that, Dixon was hurt badly in the fall and was in pain for the rest of the decathlon.

Bruce saw the fall and worried. He remembered what had happened to Jeff Bennett four years before. In the 1972 Olympics, Bennett seemed to be on his way to a certain medal. But in the hurdles, someone bumped him by accident. Bennett fell and lost valuable time. The fall was not even his fault, but it ended up robbing him of a well-deserved medal!

Avilov and Kratschmer were sure to run swiftly over the hurdles in this Olympic decathlon. Bruce

Poland's Razard Skrowronek and Bruce compete in the hurdles race.

had to make a decision. Should he run just a bit carefully and slowly, or should he go all out and risk a fall and the end of his dream? Rows of tall, white hurdles stood between him and the finish line.

Bruce's practice on his living room hurdle had not been so crazy after all. He had done it to be sure that he would not fall in the big race. But now, all those countless jumps over the living-room hurdle did not seem enough. Maybe he should have put a hurdle in every room of his apartment!

When the race started, Bruce tried to forget about falling. Instead, he concentrated on running as fast as he safely could. He must have worried some, because he ran more slowly than he had intended to. But at least he did not trip. Bruce was glad just to have the hurdles out of the way and no skinned knees from falling.

Meanwhile, Avilov and Kratschmer blazed down the track in their heats. They hardly seemed to notice that there were hurdles in their way. Avilov was proving himself a champion. After his bad luck in the first event, he could have become discouraged. But he didn't, and now he was fighting his way back into the lead.

In the discus, Bruce did not take many practice throws since his first throw was often the best. Alone in the large painted circle, he spun around and let the discus fly. True to form, his first throw sailed 160 feet (48 meters), and none of his other tosses matched it. He let go a tremendous throw on his last try, but it takes more than just a hard throw to get a discus to travel. The discus flies like a very heavy frisbee and has to be thrown just right. Since Bruce did not get the throw high enough in the air, the strength of his throw did him no good.

Bruce's two main opponents did not have good luck in the discus. Their best efforts fell far short of Bruce's mark. It was at that point that Bruce started his move to the top. Before the discus, he had been 90 points out of first place. Now he was only 9 points short. But one real danger remained: the pole vault.

Many decathlon men have a terrible time with the pole vault. Of the ten events, the pole vault is probably the hardest to learn. Besides speed and strength, it takes a great deal of coordination. (Being *coordinated* means getting your muscles to do exactly what you want them to do at the right time.)

A decathlon man cannot spend too much time learning all there is to know about the pole vault. If he does, there is no time left for practicing other events. That is where Bruce had an advantage. He had practiced hard to become a good pole vaulter *before* he ever became a "decathlete."

Even so, Bruce could not be too sure of himself. Once before, when he was pole vaulting during a large meet, everything had gone wrong. No matter what he'd done in that meet, he had felt awkward and clumsy. It would have been hard to tell from watching him that he had been a fine pole vaulter since high school. That day Bruce did not make it over the bar once! If the same thing happened now, he would not even win a bronze medal (third place). But if he made it over that bar, the rest would be easy.

Bruce picked up his long pole and turned toward the crossbar, which hung 14 feet (4.2 meters) above the ground. Funny, he thought, my big moment, and no one is here to watch! Surrounding him was a stadium of empty seats instead of cheering fans. Where were the fans? Every noon the stadium was emptied so that a new group of people would have a chance to come in and watch the afternoon performances. Bruce happened to begin vaulting at noon while the switch was taking place.

Bruce started slowly toward the bar, balancing his pole at his side. Pointing the pole straight down the runway, he ran faster and faster. Then he placed the pole in the ground and jumped. His feet did not get tangled up, and he did not feel awkward. The pole bent almost in half, then snapped Bruce up in the air. Bruce passed over the bar with room to spare!

There was no roar from the empty stands, but Bruce knew that he had done it. He would win the gold medal! But he wanted more. He wanted to finish his career with a world record. When he landed on his back, buried in the soft, gigantic mattress, he gazed

Bruce expresses his delight after hurling the discus more than 50 meters.

up at the bar still in place at 15 feet 9 inches (4.8 meters). Fifteen feet nine inches! There was no way Avilov and Kratschmer could match that. Bruce was in the lead, and he was there to stay.

In the ninth event — the javelin throw — Bruce

began by playing it safe. He threw his spear carefully so that it would be sure to land with its point in the ground. If none of his throws stuck, he would get no points. He had never had trouble with the javelin before, and he had no trouble making a good first throw. On his last two throws, Bruce was thinking about the world record. He fired his long spear far into the air and easily outdistanced the throws of his opponents. With just one event to go, Bruce Jenner was in complete control.

Throwing the javelin requires all of Bruce's concentration.

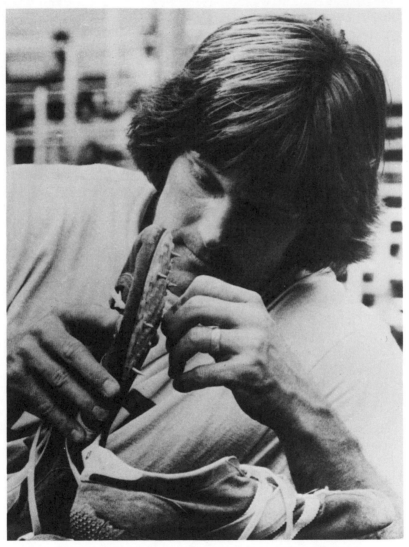

Bruce adjusts the spikes on his running shoes.

7

Avilov knew how this decathlon would end. Before the final race, he congratulated Bruce on his gold medal win. Avilov would try his best, of course, but he knew that no one could touch Bruce.

Even though the Olympics were held in Canada, the stands were packed with people from the United States. Some of them had come to Montreal just to see Bruce perform. Many had come to see other races, but they had been disappointed by American losses. Now they turned to Bruce Jenner. Surely this time they would not be disappointed.

The 1,500-meter race is the longest decathlon race (nearly a mile), and it would use up whatever strength the runners had left. It is hard enough to run a fast 1,500-meter when you are rested. But the decathlon men were very tired even *before* the race began. For two days, they had been trying to beat each other in their contest for medals. And now, in the 1,500-meter race, there weren't even separate lanes for these weary runners to run in. Everyone in each heat, including Bruce's, had to crowd together at the starting line. At the blast of the gun they each fought for a spot on the track.

Litvinenko of Russia was a tireless runner at 1,500 meters. Though he had no hope for a medal in these Olympics, he dashed to the front and soon opened up a huge lead over the rest of the runners. All Bruce had to do to insure the gold medal was to stay within a stone's throw of Avilov and Kratschmer, who were running behind Litvinenko. He ran easily behind Avilov for the first lap of the four-lap race.

Chrystie Jenner watched and cheered from the stands. She knew that Bruce wanted the world record and she knew that he had to run faster to get it. Sure enough, Bruce passed Avilov and picked up the pace. He was starting his try for the record! Though Litvinenko was far in the lead, most eyes were on Bruce. The faster he ran, the louder the crowd cheered. Not only did Bruce want the gold medal and the world record, he wanted to beat Litvinenko as well!

It seemed impossible. Litvinenko had such a huge lead! But Bruce knew that this was his last race ever. He wanted to finish like a champion.

When the bell sounded for the last lap, a magic moment in sports began. Again, the faster Bruce ran, the louder the crowd cheered. And the louder they cheered, the faster Bruce ran. The crowd had expected to see Bruce do well in the 1,500 and win the decathlon, but they had not expected anything like this!

Most distance runners are very slim. Never had the fans seen such a large and muscular man look so fast, strong, and determined near the end of a long race. Down the final stretch Bruce swept, arms and legs driving to the finish line. His eyes were fixed on Litvinenko.

In the stands, Chrystie's hoarse cheers were drowned out by the noise in the stadium as Bruce nearly caught up to Litvinenko. Bruce leaned hard into the finish line, just behind the Russian.

The stadium clock showed Bruce's time, and he knew that he had beaten the world decathlon record. He had not just beaten it; he had shattered it with 8,618 points! Bruce threw his arms high in the air and

Chrystie cries tears of happiness.

yelled for joy. The crowd roared. Many people said it was the loudest, longest cheering and clapping of the whole Olympics. Chrystie cried tears of happiness.

Bruce jogged around the track, and still the fans would not stop their noise. One of them ran onto the track and handed Bruce a small American flag. When Bruce trotted to where Chrystie sat, the police would not let her down on the track with him. But Bruce pulled Chrystie over the railing. They had shared the years of work; now they shared their joy. "We've done it!"

Bruce acknowledges cheers of the fans after breaking the world record in the decathlon and winning the gold medal.

Bruce and Chrystie share the victory that they both worked so hard for.

8

Bruce received the gold medal on the awards platform, his head still swimming from his victory. The gold medal was his! The rest of the evening, Bruce and Chrystie took turns wearing it around their necks. It was the prize that the Jenners had been wanting all this time. But it was not the only prize that Bruce won with his world-record Olympics performance. He also won world-wide attention.

Besides the thousands of spectators in the stadium at Montreal, millions had watched the magic final lap on television. People wanted to know more about this new hero. Newspaper, magazine, and television writers, as well as autograph seekers, trailed Bruce and Chrystie everywhere. They asked hundreds of questions and snapped thousands of pictures. Besides being interviewed, the Jenners appeared at dinners and award nights and on national television shows. The neighborhood kids gave Bruce and Chrystie a rousing welcome at the home of Bruce's parents. Later Bruce received the Sullivan trophy, honoring him as America's top amateur athlete of 1976.

Bruce looked and acted like a star. He was as good-looking as a movie hero, with his strong, almost perfectly shaped body and his nice smile. Besides that, he was friendly, polite, and intelligent, and he always seemed to say the right things at the right times.

Because Bruce was a star, he had an opportunity to make lots of money. Some people called him an "instant millionaire" after his gold-medal win. Not unexpectedly, the offers began pouring in soon after Montreal. Bruce was promised thousands of dollars for doing just a few minutes' work. One company would pay him to jump out of a cereal box for a commercial. Another company wanted him to do toothpaste commercials. Still another asked him to throw light bulbs as if they were javelins. It seemed like an easy way to make money.

But Bruce knew better. Other sports stars had been in the same spot before. They had not known much

The Sullivan trophy was awarded to Bruce for being the out-standing amateur athlete of 1976.

about business, and they had not thought much about how they would act once they became famous. They did not know which offers to take and which to turn down.

Bruce had planned ahead. He had decided he would not do anything that he felt was silly or not worthwhile, no matter how much money he was offered. Now that he was famous as an Olympic champion, he had to be careful. He knew that the public had a short memory and that his fame would not last forever. So Bruce decided to make wise use of his good fortune. He decided to wait for the right offers. He hired some people whom he could trust to help him make business decisions. But most important, he kept on being Bruce Jenner, the friendly young man whom everyone had seen in Montreal.

Some writers liked to call the decathlon winner "the world's greatest athlete," because the decathlon requires so many different talents. But Bruce would just shake his head when he read things like this. If only the sports writers could see him out on the golf course or watch him get hit on the head while playing tennis! Bruce realized that there was no way of knowing for sure who the world's best athlete was. But he knew that he was the world's best at the decathlon in 1976, and that was honor enough.

A new life awaited the Jenners. Before the Olympics, there was only one thing in their lives: the decathlon. Now, after the Olympics, they could relax and try out all sorts of new and exciting activities. Bruce took on work in television and commercials, and was hired by a large food company to direct their public fitness program. And now he could participate in other sports without worrying about hurting himself for the decathlon. Chrystie started work on a book and began fixing up their new home. Even Bertha settled down to the new task of raising puppies.

If you had visited the Jenners then, you would not have found a hurdle in the middle of their living room. That part of their life—chasing a gold medal—was over.

Someday, Bruce Jenner's Olympic decathlon record of 8,618 points will be broken. Perhaps that day is just around the corner. In August 1978, Francis Thompson of England jolted the sports world by scoring 8,467 points, very close to Bruce's record. Francis was only 20 years old at the time! And at the 1980 Olympics in Moscow, Daley Thompson of Great Britain came even closer to beating Bruce's Olympic record with his score of 8,495 points.

Although someone may soon top Bruce Jenner's

Chrystie, Bruce, and Bertha relax.

record-setting Olympic score, no one can ever take away the gold medal that marked the high point of his career. Bruce's long struggle with the decathlon has brought him a good living and enough thrilling memories to last a lifetime. And for his friends and family, the biggest payoff was seeing Bruce's face when he crossed the finish line for the 1,500 meters at Montreal.

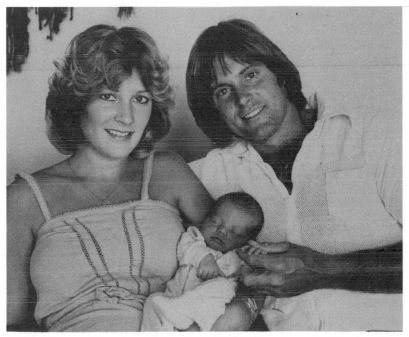

Chrystie and Bruce with their son, Burton, born in September 1978. The Jenner's second son, Michael, was born in June 1980, after the couple had decided to divorce.

OLYMPIC DECATHLON WINNERS

1912: Hugo Weislander, Sweden . . . . 5,377 points
1920: Helge Lovland, Norway . . . . 5,190 points
1924: Harold Osborn, U.S.A. . . . . 6,163 points
1928: Paavo Yrjola, Finland . . . . 6,246 points
1932: James Bausch, U.S.A. . . . . 6,588 points
1936: Glenn Morris, U.S.A. . . . . 7,310 points
1948: Bob Mathias, U.S.A. . . . . 6,386 points
1952: Bob Mathias, U.S.A. . . . . 7,887 points
1956: Milton Campbell, U.S.A. . . . . 7,937 points
1960: Rafer Johnson, U.S.A. . . . . 8,392 points
1964: Willi Holdorf, Germany . . . . 7,887 points
1968: Bill Toomey, U.S.A. . . . . 8,193 points
1972: Nikolai Avilov, U.S.S.R. . . . . 8,454 points
1976: Bruce Jenner, U.S.A. . . . . 8,618 points
1980: Daley Thompson, Great Britain . . . . 8,495 points

THE WINNERS' SCORES

EVENT	AVILOV 1972	JENNER 1976	THOMPSON 1980
100-meter (in sec.)	11.09	10.94	10.62
Long jump (in ft./in.)	25-2½	23-8½	26-3
Shot put (in ft./in.)	47-1½	50-4¼	49-10
High jump (in ft./in.)	6-11½	6-8	6-9⅞
400-meter (in sec.)	48.5	47.5	48.01
High hurdles (in sec.)	14.31	14.84	14.47
Discus (in ft./in.)	154-1½	164-1	138.7
Pole vault (in ft./in.)	14-11¼	15-9	15-5
Javelin (in ft./in.)	202-3½	224-10	210-6
1500-meter (in min./sec.)	4:22.8	4:12.3	4:39.9
Total Points	8,454	8,618	8,495

62

Index

Avilov, Nikolai: in Montreal
  Olympics, 28, 30-31, 33-34,
  35-37, 38, 43, 46, 49; in Munich
  Olympics, 8-10, 11; in world
  competition, 23

balance (in athletic ability), 21
Bell, Earl, 39
Bennett, Jeff, 41
Bertha, 28, 59, 61

Chrystie. *See* Jenner, Chrystie

decathlon: challenge of, 21;
  definition of, 10, 58; scoring
  of, 11, 29-30
discus, 11, 43-44
Dixon, Fred, 30, 31, 34, 41
Drake Relays, 15

Eugene, Oregon, 16

false start, 30, 31
400-meter race, 10, 37-38

gold medal, Olympic, 18, 25, 39
  49, 50, 55
Graceland College, 14, 19

heats, 30
high jump, 11, 35-37
hurdles, 10, 41-43

injuries, 14, 41

javelin, 11, 46-47
Jenner, Chrystie, 16, 19, 27, 28,
  50, 51-52, 55-56, 59, 61
Johnson, Rafer, 21
jumping events, 10-11

Kratschmer, Guido, 30, 31, 33-34
  35-36, 38, 43, 46

Litvinenko (Russian runner),
  50-51
long jump, 10, 11, 33-34
Montreal, Canada, 27
Olympics: in ancient Greece, 7;
  in Montreal, Canada, 25, 27,
  49; in Moscow, U.S.S.R., 59;
  in Munich, West Germany,
  8-12, 18, 41
100-meter race, 10, 29-30
1,500-meter race, 10, 50-51

pole vault, 11, 44-46

races: 400-meter, 10, 37-38;
  hurdles, 10; 100-meter, 10,
  29-30; 1,500-meter, 10, 50-51
Roberts, Dave, 39

San Jose, California, 20
scoring in decathlon competition,
  11, 16
Shorter, Frank, 39
shot put, 11, 34-35
sprint, 10
Stones, Dwight, 39
Sullivan trophy, 56

tension in Olympic competition,
  28-29, 39
Thompson, Daley, 59
Thompson, Francis, 59
throwing events, 11
Toomey, Bill, 28-29
training, 20, 23, 25, 44
try-outs for Olympics, 16, 18, 24

Weldon, L.D., 13-14
world record, decathlon, 11, 23

Yang, C. K., 21

ACKNOWLEDGMENTS: The photographs in this book are reproduced through the courtesy of: pp. 2, 6, 9, 40, 42, 54, 57, United Press International; pp. 5, 17, 22, 23, 24, 26, 32, 37, 46, 47, 48, 52, 53, 60, 61, Wide World Photos.

Cover photograph by Heinz Kluetmeier, *Sports Illustrated* © 1979 Time, Inc.

Lerner Publications Company
241 First Avenue North, Minneapolis, Minnesota 55401